CONTENTS

Scan QR codes throughout for
step-by-step pictures of each craft.

CRAFT WITH MATH!

What comes to mind when you think of math? You may think of school or equations. But did you think of crafts? Math is used to make art, games, and more! Designers find smart ways to make these items. Many creators repurpose materials. This keeps costs low and is good for the earth.

Get ready to make your own cool, Earth-friendly crafts with math!

EARTH-FRIENDLY
MATH
CRAFTS

Veronica Thompson

Lerner Publications ◆ Minneapolis

Lerner Publications Company
A division of Lerner Publishing Group, Inc.
241 First Avenue North
Minneapolis, MN 55401 USA

For reading levels and more information, look up this title at www.lernerbooks.com.

Main body text set in Avenir LT Pro 12/16.
Typeface provided by Linotype AG.

Photo Acknowledgments
The images in this book are used with the permission of: © cosmaa/Shutterstock Images, p. 1 (Earth icon); © Stilesta/Shutterstock Images, pp. 1, 3, 9, 11, 13, 15, 17, 19, 21, 23, 24, 25, 27, 28 (border design element); © narvikk/iStockphoto, p. 4 (game); © Paul Michael Hughes/Shutterstock, p. 4 (girl); © ShutterStockStudio/Shutterstock Images, pp. 5, 7; © absolut/Shutterstock Images, p. 6 (top); © addkm/Shutterstock Images, p. 6 (boots); © Enrique Ramos/Shutterstock Images, p. 6 (shirt); © Sergey Nivens/Shutterstock Images, p. 7 (background); Veronica Thompson, pp. 8, 9 (top), 9 (center), 9 (bottom), 10, 11 (top), 11 (center), 11 (bottom), 12, 13 (top), 13 (center), 13 (bottom), 14, 15 (top), 15 (center), 15 (bottom), 16, 17 (top), 17 (center), 17 (bottom), 18, 19 (top), 19 (center), 19 (bottom), 20, 21 (top), 21 (center top), 21 (center bottom), 21 (bottom), 22, 23 (top), 23 (center), 23 (bottom), 24 (top), 24 (center), 24 (bottom), 25 (top), 25 (bottom), 26, 27 (top), 27 (center), 27 (bottom), 28 (top), 28 (center), 28 (bottom); © ChaiyaTN/Shutterstock Images, p. 29 (top); © Iasha/Shutterstock Images, p. 29 (bottom); © RyanJLane/iStockphoto, p. 30; © mastersky/iStockphoto, p. 31; © Bozena Fulawka/Shutterstock Images, p. 32 (top); Courtesy Veronica Thompson, p. 32 (bottom); © Curly Pat/Shutterstock Images, pp. 9, 11, 13, 15, 17, 19, 21, 23, 24, 25, 27, 28 (design element).

Front cover: Veronica Thompson (main); © cosmaa/Shutterstock Images (Earth icon)
Back cover: © Curly Pat/Shutterstock Images (background design element); © Stilesta/Shutterstock Images (border design element)

Library of Congress Cataloging-in-Publication Data

Names: Thompson, Veronica, 1989– author.
Title: Earth-friendly math crafts / by Veronica Thompson.
Description: Minneapolis, MN : Lerner Publications, [2019] | Series: Green STEAM | Includes bibliographical references and index. | Audience: Ages 12-18.
Identifiers: LCCN 2017059750 (print) | LCCN 2017053544 (ebook) | ISBN 9781541524248 (eb pdf) | ISBN 9781541524194 (lb : alk. paper) | ISBN 9781541527812 (pb : alk. paper)
Subjects: LCSH: Handicraft—Juvenile literature. | Mathematics—Juvenile literature.
Classification: LCC TT160 (print) | LCC TT160 .T36727 2019 (ebook) | DDC 745.5—dc23

LC record available at https://lccn.loc.gov/2017059750

Manufactured in the United States of America
1-44507-34763-4/24/2018

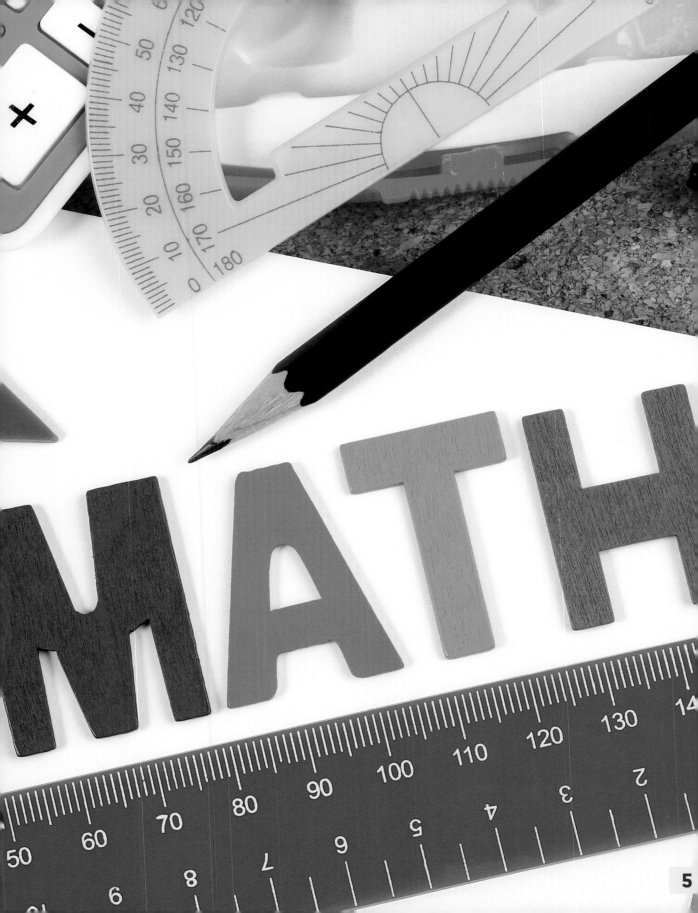

CHOOSING MATERIALS

When you're gathering things to repurpose, it's okay to be picky. For example, avoid badly crushed cardboard boxes and paper with grease or liquid stains. Ask an adult before reusing something that's not in the recycling bin. The item may be serving another purpose already!

CLEAN MACHINE

Repurposed materials may be dirty. Give these materials a good scrub before you craft with them! Rinse off and wipe down old rain boots and wash and dry clothing items before using them in a project.

STAY SAFE!

Some crafts in this book require the use of
hot or sharp tools and strong paints. Ask
for an adult's help when using these items:
- craft knife
- hot glue gun
- latex paint

COLOR-BLOCKED RAIN BOOTS

Use fractions to give old boots and leftover paint new life! Finding a use for leftover paint keeps it from polluting the earth.

MATERIALS
~ old rubber boots
~ ruler
~ chalk
~ painter's tape
~ leftover latex paint
~ stir stick
~ paintbrush

Scan the QR code for more photos.

1 Measure the height of each boot from the bottom of the heel to the top of the boot. Divide the number by three.

2 Measure and mark the top third of each boot using the ruler and chalk. Wrap painter's tape around each boot **horizontally** so the tape's top edge meets the chalk lines.

3 Stir the leftover paint. Carefully paint the top third of each boot. Let the paint dry.

4 Repeat step 3 to add more coats of paint if needed.

5 Peel off the tape slowly to reveal your mathematically improved boots!

PUNNY MATH SHIRT

Math can be funny two (get it?)! Update an old T-shirt into a wearable joke that will make your math teacher smile. Search "math jokes for kids" online to find a funny saying. Or make up your own!

Dear Math,

Solve your own problems.

MATERIALS
- ~ computer
- ~ word-processing program
- ~ printer
- ~ printer paper
- ~ old light-colored T-shirt
- ~ tape
- ~ paint
- ~ liquid fabric medium
- ~ thin-tipped paintbrushes

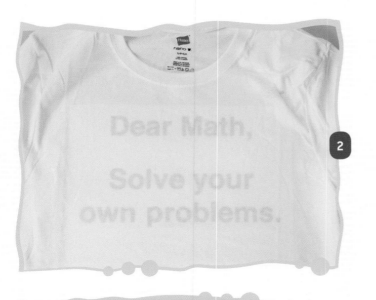

1 Type your saying in a word-processing program. Enlarge the type so the text takes up most of the page. Print the page.

2 Lay the T-shirt flat and slide the sheet of paper inside it. You should be able to see the words through the shirt. If you can't, move to work under a brighter light. Center the saying and tape the paper in place inside the shirt.

3 Mix equal amounts of paint and **liquid fabric medium**.

4 Carefully paint the words onto the T-shirt using the printout as a guide. When the paint dries, your creation is ready to wear!

SIMPLE SCALE

What's the difference between size and weight? Repurpose an old paper towel tube into a scale to help you find out.

MATERIALS

- colorful duct tape
- recycled paper towel tube
- shoebox lid
- scissors
- wooden dowel
- hot glue gun & glue sticks
- 2 small paper cups
- hole punch
- string
- ruler
- rubber bands
- candies, toys, or other small items

STEM Takeaway

Scales measure how much the Earth's gravity pulls an object down. This measurement is the object's weight.

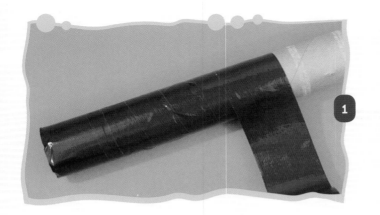

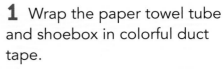

1 Wrap the paper towel tube and shoebox in colorful duct tape.

2 Cut two **notches** in one end of the paper towel tube. The notches should be across from each other. Make each notch as wide as the wooden dowel.

3 Glue the uncut end of the paper towel tube to the center of the shoebox lid. Hold the tube in place until the glue dries.

4 Punch two holes near the rim of each paper cup. The holes in each cup should be across from each other.

5 Cut a 4-inch (10 cm) length of string. Tie its ends to the holes in one cup to form a handle. Repeat with the other cup.

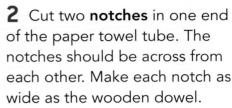

6 Wrap a rubber band around each end of the dowel. Then set the center of the dowel into the paper towel tube notches. Hang one cup on each dowel end. Fill the cups with different combinations of the items you gathered. What happens?

SWAP IT!

Swap the paper cups for recycled plastic ones. You can also use paint to decorate the scale pieces instead of duct tape.

DIVISION STRING ART

Division makes a geometric web of string in this pretty piece of wall art. Use math to make the design complex or simple!

MATERIALS
~ marker
~ measuring tape
~ repurposed basketry wood hoop
~ paint in a variety of colors
~ paintbrushes
~ scissors
~ recycled string

OPTIONAL
~ decorations such as paper flowers, ribbon, or cards

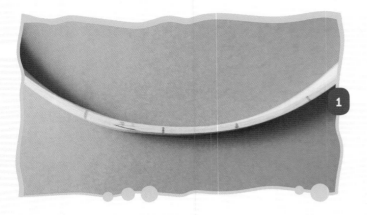

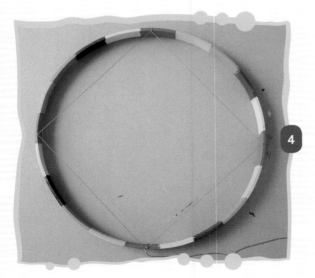

1 Use a marker and measuring tape to divide the hoop into twenty equal parts. Begin by dividing it into quarters. Then divide each quarter into five equal sections.

2 Paint the sections different colors. Once the paint dries, number the sections from 1 to 20.

3 Tie a piece of string several feet long around the middle of section 1.

4 Count five sections over and tie the string to the hoop again. Repeat this twice more in the same direction. You should be back to section 1. This is because the count of five divides evenly into twenty. Tie the string around the hoop again.

5 Repeat step 3 but count by sections of three. This count won't bring you back to section 1, as three does not divide evenly into twenty. But that's okay! Just begin another count from a new section.

6 Try different counts to create a webbed pattern. If you run out of string, tie more onto the loose end.

SWAP IT!
Swap the basketry hoop for a ring cut from a recycled plastic lid.

EQUATION INVASION GAME

Turn a recycled project poster into a themed math game. Play with family or friends. Use addition and subtraction to win!

MATERIALS

- recycled poster board
- marker
- paint
- paintbrushes
- recycled paper
- paper punch or scissors
- deck of cards without kings, queens, jacks, and aces

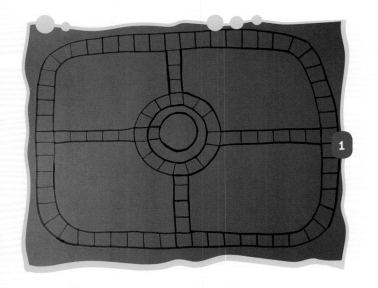

1 Draw a board game path on the poster board. Divide the path into equal-sized spaces.

2 Pick a space on the board and paint and label it with a plus sign. When players land here, they will draw a numbered card and move forward that number of spaces.

3 Paint a minus sign in another space. When players land here, they will draw a card and move backward that number. Repeat steps 2 and 3 around the board.

4 Add the word "even" to some spaces. Do the same with the word "odd." When players land on one of these spaces, they must continue to draw cards until they get one that is either an even or odd number. They will move forward that number of spaces.

5 Choose a theme and decorate the board!

6 Cut or punch different colors of recycled paper into shapes. Use these as game pieces.

SWAP IT!
You can swap the deck of cards for dice.

17

SMALL
SURPRISE CUBE

Measure and divide to turn recycled card stock into colorful little cubes! These boxes can hold small surprises or secret notes.

STEM Takeaway
Cubes are three-dimensional shapes. Their three dimensions are height, width, and depth.

MATERIALS
~ recycled card stock
~ ruler
~ scissors
~ tape
~ recycled paper scraps

OPTIONAL
~ crayons or markers

1 Fold a sheet of card stock in half crosswise, then once more the same way. Open the card stock. The **creases** should divide it into fourths.

2 Fold the card stock in thirds vertically, then unfold. The card stock should be divided into twelve squares.

3 If your card stock has images or type on one side, keep these faceup. This way, they will be hidden inside the box. Cut the creases along the long sides. Leave the center row of squares intact.

4 Fold the far left column up, bending its tabs in to make a U shape. Fold the tabs from the next column up and tape them to the sides of the U.

5 Fold the next column up and toward the U. Tuck the flaps in and tape the sides together.

6 The remaining column is the lid. Fold and tuck it into the top of the cube.

7 Cut the paper scraps into confetti and fill your cube with them. Then place a surprise inside for a friend or family member!

GEOMETRIC EMOJI PROPS

Many emoji details are made up of geometric shapes. Use recycled paper and math to make photo prop faces!

MATERIALS
- ~ recycled construction paper in different colors
- ~ protractor
- ~ pencil
- ~ scissors
- ~ glue
- ~ ruler
- ~ dowels or popsicle sticks

EYE ROLL EMOJI
- ~ 2 large circles
- ~ 2 small circles
- ~ 1 thin rectangle

HEART EYES EMOJI
- ~ 4 small circles
- ~ 2 small triangles
- ~ 1 large half circle

CRYING EMOJI
- ~ 1 circle
- ~ 2 half circles
- ~ 2 long rectangles
- ~ 2 short rectangles
- ~ 1 small half circle

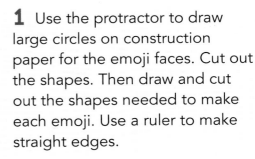

1 Use the protractor to draw large circles on construction paper for the emoji faces. Cut out the shapes. Then draw and cut out the shapes needed to make each emoji. Use a ruler to make straight edges.

EYE ROLL EMOJI

2 Glue the rectangle on the face as the mouth.

3 Glue the large circles to the face as eyes. Glue a smaller circle at the top of each eye to form the eye roll!

HEART EYES EMOJI

4 Glue the triangles to the face where the eyes should go. Top each triangle with two circles to form hearts.

5 Add the half circle as the smile.

CRYING EMOJI

6 Glue the circle to the face as a mouth. Add the small half circle as teeth.

7 Glue the large half circles to the face as eyes and the short rectangles as eyebrows. Add the long rectangles to the bottom of the eyes as tears.

8 Glue a dowel or popsicle stick to the back of each emoji as a handle. Use the faces as props while **posing** for photos!

MULTIPLICATION COASTER

Practice multiplication to make a cool and cozy coaster of colorful arrays!

MATERIALS
~ leftover loose wool
~ sponge
~ blunt darning or embroidery needle
~ protractor
~ string

STEM Takeaway
Multiplying the number of items on any two sides will produce the complete number of items in the array.

1 To create a felted wool ball, first take a bit of loose wool and roll it between your hands into a loose, fluffy ball.

2 Place the ball on a clean sponge. Begin poking the ball with the needle, rotating it as you work. Soon, a slightly tighter ball should form.

3 Keep rotating and poking the ball until it is about one quarter of its original size.

4 Repeat steps 1 through 3 to make many felted balls.

Multiplication Coaster
continued on next page

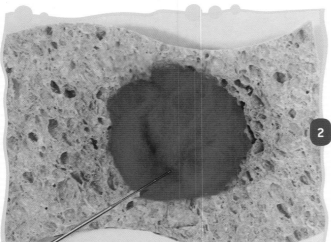

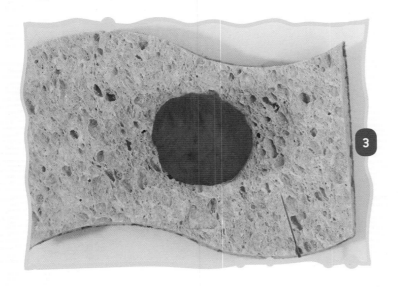

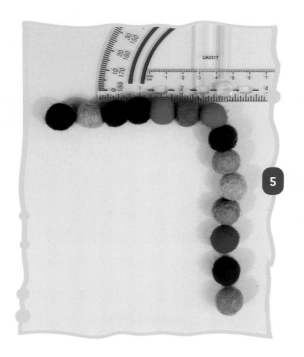

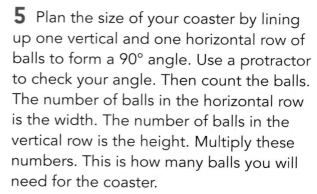

5 Plan the size of your coaster by lining up one vertical and one horizontal row of balls to form a 90° angle. Use a protractor to check your angle. Then count the balls. The number of balls in the horizontal row is the width. The number of balls in the vertical row is the height. Multiply these numbers. This is how many balls you will need for the coaster.

6 Thread your needle with string. Tie a double knot at the end.

7 Pass the needle through the center of one ball. Repeat to create a row matching the number of the coaster's height.

8 Push the needle through the top of the last ball so the needle comes out its bottom.

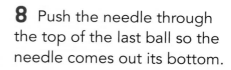

9 Add one ball to the string. Then push the needle through the right side of this ball, so it comes out on the ball's left. You have begun a new row!

10 Add more balls to the second row until it is as long as the first.

11 When you have completed the second row, repeat step 8. Then repeat step 9, but so the thread comes out the ball's right side.

12 Repeat steps 7 through 11 to complete the array.

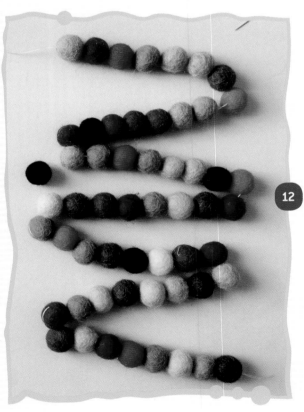

13 Run your needle and thread through each felt ball along the array's **perimeter**. Tie a knot at the last ball and trim the extra string. Your coaster is ready for use!

SHADOW SHAPES LENS

Use an old toilet paper tube to turn a flashlight into a geometric shape projector!

MATERIALS
~ recycled toilet paper tube
~ scissors
~ tape
~ recycled construction paper in a dark color
~ pencil or marker
~ craft knife
~ flashlight with batteries

1 Cut the toilet paper tube into three rings.

2 Cut one ring open. **Overlap** its ends a bit to make a slightly smaller ring and tape it together.

3 Fit the smaller ring about halfway into one of the other rings. Tape the pieces together.

4 Trace both ends of the connected tube from step 3 onto construction paper. Cut out the circles. One should be slightly larger than the other.

5 Draw geometric shapes in the center of each circle. Leave a little space between the shapes and the circles' edges.

Shadow Shapes Lens continued on next page

6 Have an adult cut out the shapes inside each circle using a craft knife. The circles with cutouts are lenses.

7 Tape the smaller lens to the smaller end of the connected tubes from step 3.

8 Tape the larger lens to the third ring from step 1.

9 Stand the connected tubes so the lenses face up. Fit the tube from step 8 over them, with its lens faceup too. Tape the pieces together where they meet to make a long tube.

10 Tape the tube on top of a flashlight's lens, with the cardboard lenses facing out.

11 Turn on the flashlight in a dark room. Your cardboard tube lens will make bright geometric shapes on the wall or ceiling!

ODDS & ENDS

Craft materials and a little creativity can give new life to all kinds of old or recycled materials. What else can you repurpose?

CAN TABS

Paint tabs from old cans different colors. Arrange the tabs in an array and string them together to make a patterned woven placemat.

PAPER

Cut recycled paper scraps into geometric shapes of the same size. Glue or tape matching pieces together to make colorful 3-D shapes!

BROKEN CALCULATORS

Have an adult help you remove the buttons from a non-working calculator. Glue the buttons to string or wire to make numbered keychains or jewelry.

OLD CDS OR DVDS

Use a ruler and marker to divide an old CD or DVD into triangular sections. Paint each section. Then hang the disc as decoration!

PIZZA BOX LID

Use a ruler to measure a pizza box lid into even squares as a checkerboard. Use recycled plastic lids or bottle caps as game pieces.

GLOSSARY

arrays: objects or numbers arranged in orderly rows and columns

complex: very complicated

creases: folds or lines

creativity: the use of the imagination to think of new ideas

emoji: a small image used to express an emotion in electronic communication

equations: mathematical statements in which one set of numbers is equal to another

geometric: of or relating to simple shapes, such as triangles, circles, or squares

horizontally: in a way that is straight and level, parallel to the ground

liquid fabric medium: a liquid that creates a waterproof fabric paint when mixed with craft paint

notches: V-shaped cuts or nicks on the edge of something

overlap: to extend over or partly cover something

perimeter: the distance around the outside edge of a shape or area

posing: taking a position and staying there so you can be photographed

prop: something used in creating or enhancing a desired effect

repurpose: to give a new purpose or use

FURTHER INFORMATION

BOOKS

Lim, Annalees. *Recycling Crafts.*
New York: Gareth Stevens Publishing, 2014.
Discover cool crafts you can make from recycled items you have at home!

Marsico, Katie. *Kitchen Math.*
Minneapolis: Lerner Publications, 2015.
Put your math skills to work measuring and dividing ingredients to make all sorts of recipes!

Ward, Robin A. *Math + Art = Fun: Activities for Discovering Mathematical Magic in Modern Art.*
Houston: Bright Sky Press, 2011.
Examine famous artworks to learn how math was used to make them! Then follow instructions to make your own similar work of art.

WEBSITES

The Crafty Crow: Math Crafts
http://www.thecraftycrow.net/math/
Browse through bright photos of completed crafts made with math. Click the links to find instructions on how to make each one!

PBS: Math Crafts for Kids
http://www.pbs.org/parents/crafts-for
-kids/category/learning/math/
These math crafts are fun and simple!
Easy-to-follow step-by-step instructions are paired with photos.

The STEM Laboratory: 50 Genius STEM Activities for Kids
https://thestemlaboratory.com/stem
-activities-for-kids/
Find a huge list of links leading to directions for making amazing math crafts!

INDEX

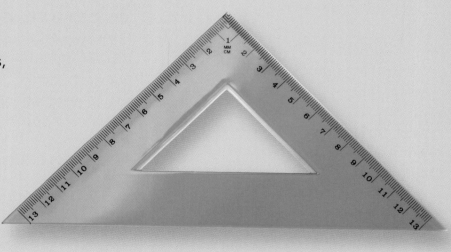

ABOUT THE AUTHOR/ PHOTOGRAPHER

Veronica Thompson lives in a little brownstone in Brooklyn, New York, with her two puppies and wonderful husband. She spends her days crafting for her website, makescoutdiy.com, and building websites.